HOW TO SAY NO TO ALCOHOL

KEITH MCNEILL is a journalist who gave up drinking six years ago and has encountered at first hand the problems of being teetotal in a world constantly pressurizing people to drink. He is married, and lives in Berkshire.

Overcoming Common Problems Series

The ABC of Eating
Coping with anorexia, bulimia and
compulsive eating
JOY MELVILLE

Acne
How it's caused and how to cure it
PAUL VAN RIEL

An A–Z of Alternative Medicine
BRENT Q. HAFEN AND KATHRYN J.
FRANDSEN

Arthritis
Is your suffering really necessary?
DR WILLIAM FOX

Birth Over Thirty
SHEILA KITZINGER

Body Language
How to read others' thoughts by their gestures
ALLAN PEASE

Calm Down
How to cope with frustration and anger
DR PAUL HAUCK

Common Childhood Illnesses
DR PATRICIA GILBERT

Coping with Depression and Elation
DR PATRICK McKEON

Curing Arthritis–The Drug-free Way
MARGARET HILLS

Depression
DR PAUL HAUCK

Divorce and Separation
ANGELA WILLANS

Enjoying Motherhood
DR BRUCE PITT

The Epilepsy Handbook
SHELAGH McGOVERN

Everything You Need to Know about Shingles
DR ROBERT YOUNGSON

**Everything You Need to Know about Contact
Lenses**
DR ROBERT YOUNGSON

**Everything You Need to Know about Your
Eyes**
DR ROBERT YOUNGSON

Family First Aid and Emergency Handbook
DR ANDREW STANWAY

Fears and Phobias
What they are and how to overcome them
DR TONY WHITEHEAD

Feverfew
A traditional herbal remedy for migraine and
arthritis
DR STEWART JOHNSON

Fight Your Phobia and Win
DAVID LEWIS

Fit Kit
DAVID LEWIS

Flying Without Fear
TESSA DUCKWORTH AND DAVID
MILLER

Goodbye Backache
DR DAVID IMRIE WITH COLLEEN
DIMSON

Guilt
Why it happens and how to overcome it
DR VERNON COLEMAN

How to Bring Up your Child Successfully
DR PAUL HAUCK

How to Control your Drinking
DRS MILLER AND MUNOZ

How to Cope with Stress
DR PETER TYRER

Overcoming Common Problems Series

Overcoming Common Problems Series

Overcoming Common Problems

HOW TO SAY NO
TO ALCOHOL

Keith McNeill

SHELDON PRESS
LONDON

First published in Great Britain in 1986 by
Sheldon Press, SPCK, Marylebone Road, London NW1 4DU

British Library Cataloguing in Publication Data

McNeill, Keith
   How to say no to alcohol. — (Overcoming
   common problems)
   1. Alcoholism — Treatment   2. Self-
   care, Health
   I. Title II. Series
   616.86'106   RC565

   ISBN 0-85969-514-X
   ISBN 0-85969-515-8 Pbk

Typeset by Deltatype, Ellesmere Port
Printed in Great Britain by
Richard Clay (The Chaucer Press) Ltd,
Bungay, Suffolk.

To Ruth

Contents

PART II

Introduction

I began the affair when I was seventeen. It was a ten-year nightmare. And now it's over and there's no going back.

I see now that I should never have started on my black romance. The tell-tale signs were there, right at the beginning, but I ignored them. I was being seduced and it felt good, exciting and grown-up. She captivated and entranced me and I danced away long nights with her. She held me in her arms and I was trapped, and it took a great deal of determination to break free.

I say 'she' but my mistress and companion for all those years had no sex, no shape, no form. You couldn't see or touch her but she was there all right. At first just a small image, flirting, lurking in the background, walking in the shadows of my life, but in the last years a giant bloated monster, towering above me, filling all my waking thoughts every moment of the day. Until one day I said 'get out'. And this time I really meant it.

You see, my monster was alcohol and that is what this book is all about—how to say no to alcohol—how to send this monster packing. It can be done quite easily; just follow some simple rules, stick to a plan and wave the monster goodbye.

PART I

1

How Not To Give Up

It can't be stressed too much that in order to give up drinking you've got to have a plan. There's no point in just crossing your fingers and hoping it will all work out.

Of course all it takes to stop drinking is never to have another drink. And all that takes is to keep on refusing them. And all that takes is will-power. That's all very well. But doing it with will-power and nothing else is doing it the *hard* way. I know because that's the way I did it. I recommend it to nobody.

When I gave up drinking I just stopped. I had no plan, no idea. I just woke up one morning and said 'never again'. Luckily I survived, but at first it seemed touch and go . . .

The problem is time, and what to do with it. Time on your hands. Time, bringing with it boredom—acheing, numbing, soul-destroying boredom—at first. Why? Because you forget what you used to do with yourself before you started drinking. And now there's a great hole in your life where drink used to be.

The first day is the worst. It hits you like a cold shower, like a bereavement, an old friend who isn't there anymore and isn't going to be ever again. Taking it in sends a cold shiver down the spine and a feeling of panic sets in. (The old friend is really a bitter enemy but in those first five minutes it doesn't seem like it.)

My panic set in at noon on the big day. Four hours into the first day of the rest of my life and it was time to go to the pub. But wait! Hold it! There's not going to be any more slipping off to the bar for a couple of hours' drinking every lunchtime, no more pints of beer, cheese rolls and endless chatter . . . Well, what are you supposed to do when you don't go drinking? I had only just given up and life had come to a halt.

I slumped into a chair and stared blindly out of the window.

'Is it really worth giving up?' I heard myself asking. Surely it would be better to concentrate on cutting down, drinking halves instead of pints and educating myself to become a sensible social drinker. In the first moments I was being drawn to the pub like a compass needle to a magnet. It was make or break. I had to stand my ground and push away all thoughts of going to the pub.

What I should have done was planned this new morning. I should have organized a diversion that kept me away from the pub and genuinely occupied me, like a game of golf, or a morning's fishing, or I should have helped someone else with their work. I should have planned it so I went to the pub for the last 20 minutes of the session. Just long enough to cope with not drinking. But I didn't.

Health was the keyword I was using to fight the monster. My new life would bring about a healthy body, a healthy mind and a healthy and productive lifestyle. From now on things were going to be different. I would have a routine to go with my new resolution. It was with this in mind that I had started the day with a few Canadian Air Force exercises on the bedroom carpet, then downstairs to a grapefruit and yoghurt breakfast and a jog around the block.

That was in the morning. Three hours later I was sitting in an armchair staring out of the window. I must do something, I thought. I put on my newly-bought tracksuit and set off to jog to the paper shop.

I should add, for anyone who is wondering why I'm not killing time by doing a spot of honest work, that I had given up drinking on a Sunday. Sunday of all days. The one day of the week when almost everybody goes out at lunchtime and gets high, and then spends the rest of the day sleeping it off in front of the television. Here was a day devoted entirely to eating and drinking and I didn't drink. (If man had created the world the Book of Genesis would have read: 'In six days man created the earth and everything in it and on the seventh he went to the pub to celebrate.')

6

It was the second jog I'd had that day and my arrival at the newsagents would have killed anyone with a weak heart. I burst through the doorway red-faced, doubled up and sucking in air with an eerie whistling noise. Five minutes later I felt fit enough to risk talking and ordered three of the fattest Sunday papers they had. I walked home.

Like everyone who starts afresh I had an image of what it would be like. Jogging, trendy Sunday papers and orange juice fitted that image. I sat down in the front room, piled the papers on the table and spread the first one out in front of me. I settled back. 'Who needs a drink?' I asked myself.

Ten minutes later I was staring at the clock.

I took down a book and started to read. Head down, I painstakingly pored over a dozen pages, deliberately averting my eyes from the clock. A chapter later I looked up triumphantly – the clock hands had hardly moved. I had a bath, a good long soak and came back downstairs. Time had barely dragged its weary self forward. A jog, a bath, a bit of a book and the papers had taken up well under an hour. It was awful.

My problem was I wanted instant results. I thought that just giving up was somehow like waving a magic wand.

Down at my local bar time would race by. In the pub there was never enough time. No sooner had you got your drinks in and chatted to a few people and the landlord was seeing everyone out. Back at home those couple of hours that first day seemed interminable; each hour felt like four.

It took me a long time to get used to those extra hours I now have each day. Today I enjoy the time I used to throw away in dingy bars and ale houses. That time is a bonus, a treat denied the drinker. What do I do with it? I read, play squash, go for a walk, cook, listen to music, meet real friends, talk sense, the list is endless. Nowadays, not drinking is such a joy I could never go back.

Giving up alcohol means entering into a completely new world, a world parallel with the drinking one but utterly different. Once you have entered this land of the teetotal, life

7

can never be the same again. At first it seems difficult, even horrible, but pretty soon it becomes a land you never want to leave.

Quitting drinking changes your life because of the reactions of everyone else and the amount of 'social' drinking people indulge in. It was not until I stopped that I realized just how much people drink. Alcohol is everywhere. No occasion is too small for a drink and a celebration is inconceivable without someone opening a bottle.

With all this drink around I swiftly realized that avoiding it is impossible and should not be attempted. You have to live without alcohol but alongside it. (The only way to avoid drink's influence is to pack up and go and live in a cave somewhere, and even there you would probably find your store of apples went rotten and turned into cider!)

Saying 'I don't drink' is like announcing you have only got six months to live. People are terribly interested but don't want to come too close to you. The effect on the hard drinkers is always the same. At first they are stumped but this quickly turns to suspicion. That first smile hardens and there is a frostiness in the eyes; they have just lost a potential drinking partner and people who do not drink are weird—everyone knows that. But their curiosity is aroused: what is the matter with you? This attitude of the big drinkers—that all people who don't drink are in some way pathetic—is just something you have to learn to live with.

Coping with a non-drinker is a real problem for the drinking classes. They have no idea how to and quite frankly couldn't care less. They regard the teetotaller as only marginally more interesting than the earthworm. So when you reject alcohol your life inevitably changes. Old haunts, old customs and even old friends quickly lose their appeal if that appeal was centred on drinking. These faces and places, so familiar, are dropped by the newly converted abstainer just as a lizard sheds an old skin it no longer has any use for. A reformed drinker soon finds out who his real friends are.

Soon after I gave up drinking people kept coming up to me

and saying things like: 'I do admire you, I could never do it. I have so many pressures I just have to unwind', or 'I could do it for most of the time but I would miss that glass of lager on a hot summer afternoon, sitting in the garden or watching the cricket.'

Pretty soon I began to slip into mourning. 'Curse this great sacrifice I've made', I said. I began daydreaming scenes I would never again be able to enjoy—the dark foaming pint of Blue Dragon XXX gulped down as I watched that Sunday afternoon cricket match, or the two fingers of Arkansas Ambulance 100° proof bourbon poured out to help me unwind at the end of a hard working day.

What rubbish. I was regretting never again being able to do things I didn't do anyway. It's all part of the myth of drink in which we associate alcohol with fun and laughter, girls in pretty crinolines, punting on the river, cricket on the green, romance in the rhododendrons and perpetual summer. Life isn't like that—drink or no drink.

That first Sunday lunchtime when I didn't go out for a drink I remained dejected until the bars closed and the pressure was off. I should have been happy but all I felt was a bit fed up.

I saw the morning as a period of self-denial, I saw it as losing something. But I was wrong. I had scored my first victory. I had stood up for myself and come through a winner. It was a small victory but it was a success. The Chinese say that a journey of a thousand miles starts with a single step. I had taken my first step, I should have been happy. Always think positive.

That evening, I remember, I went to the cinema. It was the easiest way of keeping out of the pub. Afterwards I bought a take-away meal, came home and watched some television. The day had been a success. I had not had a drink. I knew from that day on that I never wanted to drink again.

I also knew that I could not spend the rest of my life in a cinema. In order to lead a normal life I sometimes had to go where the beer and wine flowed. I would have to go to pubs, to meet friends in bars, to meet business colleagues for lunch, to go to weddings, parties, to eat in restaurants, to go to stag nights and to celebrate birthdays.

I did all these things and four years later I haven't had a drink. To survive as a non-drinker in a drinking world I had to learn to say no and to keep on saying no. The following chapters will show you how to make it easier to learn that lesson and realize there is nothing wrong in saying no to alcohol.

The sooner everyone realizes that, the better!

2
Look in the Mirror

This is a test everyone should do every couple of years, whether they are worried about drinking or not. The point is to take stock of yourself and see just how you are developing.

Imagine you are a wide-eyed 15-year-old again. Now go and look in the mirror with those fresh young 15-year-old eyes. What do you see? Does it make you happy, or would you rather look away? Is this how you thought you'd look when you grew up—how has it turned out so far?

I took this test more than four years ago and I failed. I looked in the mirror and what I saw betrayed that young teenager I had been. If he had come and stood beside me I wouldn't have wanted him to recognize me. I was flabby, unfit and unhappy about it.

Today I took that test again and I passed. Four years after turning my back on drink I can look straight into the mirror with pride.

Giving up drinking was the best thing I ever did. Instead of suffering because I can't have a drink, pulling long faces and feeling bored, not drinking has flooded me with confidence. I am a new man—and it's great.

Why do we drink?

One of the main reasons why we drink is to give ourselves confidence, in the belief that a few glasses oils the tongue and sets us at ease—especially with strangers.

There are, of course, plenty of other reasons: loneliness, wanting to please others, being frightened of feeling left out, using drink as bridge between each other, drinking to impress, or just wanting to shut out the world in an alcoholic haze. And it's often not just one of these reasons but a combination. We

11

are all at times a bit lonely, frightened, unsure of what to say, anxious about meeting people—friends as well as strangers—and we turn to the bottle to help us over these fears and stumblings. It is a short step from this to using the bottle whenever life 'closes in'. Then you have a problem, because life can 'close in' at any time. It doesn't help to drink. For example, the lonely woman sitting in her house with her memories turns to drink as a comfort—but she is still lonely and lost. The young adolescent, stammering his awkward, gawky way to a first date, reaches for a drink to straighten his words—but in his heart he is as shy as ever. The tired businessman forgets his office worries by blurring them out with several large nightcaps—but his fears are only put off for a couple of hours and, in the morning, they return.

How many people always have a drink before chatting someone up at a disco, or go to the pub for a 'loosener' on the way to a party? Quite a lot. For the big drinkers, going out for an evening and not drinking is like going out for an evening without their clothes on. They just wouldn't do it. Like their clothes, they see alcohol as essential. This is of course a myth. They are using drink as a crutch, scared they will fail without it.

Watch the changes day by day

Far from helping, alcohol is a hindrance. Throw away the crutch and you'll realize you don't need it. Drink isn't a passport to success and happiness; these come when you stop drinking. In just a couple of months after giving up, you can change from an overweight, slobby, depressed drinker into a fit, slim, healthy-looking teetotaller. The change doesn't take place overnight, but with every day things get better and better, and the transformation is wonderful. And that's how it is for anyone who decides to give up drinking.

Too many people think that sober means straight. They're wrong—being sober is being smart. Only when you give up drinking do you see this. So do it now, swap beer for attractiveness, swap drunkenness for confidence.

Be honest, go and have a look in that mirror and if you don't like what you see do something about it—today.

If you think you can't, you're wrong. All it takes is you. Each time you say no it gets easier and easier, until it becomes part of your life, an automatic unthinking response. As natural and as easy as breathing.

On the face of it, saying no seems such an easy thing, politely declining a drink with a few well-chosen words and a gracious nod. Simple. So why write about it? Because it isn't like that. Especially if you are weak-willed, half-hearted, addicted or just plain scared, 'no' can seem the hardest word to say. But saying no *is* very easy, if you plan what you are doing, stick to your guns, take command and refuse to give in. Sounds a lot? Well, it isn't.

Accept you are different

Saying no is hard because the pressures to drink in today's society are enormous. Putting it bluntly, the biggest pressure is that not drinking means you are different from the rest. Despite what we think, we are a uniform society, extremely convention-al, and we don't like people who are not like us. We are prejudiced against them—so it is hard to become one of the different people. But don't despair. The situation is very, very far from being hopeless. Admit honestly to yourself that you are committed to not drinking and that because of this you are different.

Once you accept it, realize that being different is rather special and enjoy it. Don't feel small, feel big. You are no longer one of the crowd—you know your own mind and go your own way. It is this feeling of independence that is the key to saying no. When you say no you are moving out of the mainstream, not into some horrible little backwater but on to the crest of a wave, a wave that will carry you into new exciting waters.

Say no, and keep saying no, and pretty soon you won't think twice about it.

13

3
The Pub

The first time you go into a pub after giving up drinking presents enormous difficulties. But it does become easier with practice. The biggest problem the new non-drinker has is coping with being different.

You walk into a pub, eyes down, shoulders hunched, and shuffle nervously to the bar where you order an orange juice (it is always an orange juice) and then you stand there sheepishly sipping it and feeling hopelessly out of place. It is as if you are the only human in a room full of Martians. After five minutes one of your friends walks over and asks why you are standing there like a lemon, drinking orange juice.

Thirty minutes later, your mind screaming but outwardly calm, you casually as possible order a drink. There are smiles all around and shouts of 'knew it wouldn't last' and plenty of back-slapping. So, in for a penny in for a pound, you get drunk and over in the corner the hideous monster, drink, grins as her victim returns.

But that is not the way to do it. That is not the way to say no in a pub.

Take command of the situation

The problem is that people who used to like a good stiff drink feel thoroughly foolish standing in a pub with a glass of orange juice in their hand. They also don't see the point of being there in the first place if they're not drinking.

The answer is to take command. March into a pub head up and determined not to drink and not to be ashamed of it. Don't go to pieces as you walk through the doors, but run through what you are about to do a couple of times in your mind and make absolutely sure of yourself before going inside.

14

At the bar don't order an orange juice. The only use for this horrible sticky stuff is as a mixer with large quantities of vodka to make something called a Screwdriver by Manhattan bar staff, a very over-priced alcoholic concoction that has no place in this book.

There are plenty of non-alcoholic drinks available in a pub. Make a big thing out of ordering them; make them part of the fun of not drinking. Don't just ask for a tonic water in a tiny glass.

Here are a few suggestions. In a large balloon-shaped glass put three ice cubes and a measure of lime juice, and top up with tonic and a slice of lemon. Or use the same recipe but instead of tonic top up with American or dry ginger.

A Virgin Mary is a Bloody Mary without the vodka. Take a tall glass and add ice cubes, tabasco, Worcester sauce, tomato juice and a slice of lemon. Delicious on a hot day. In winter leave out the ice and add an extra drop of tabasco.

Grapefruit juice is nice with lemonade or soda water.

Joking apart, orange juice is not recommended because after just one or two glasses it tastes too sickly and cloying. But if orange juice is your drink it can be lightened by mixing with lemonade or soda, or for something quite different mix a single orange juice with a large bitter lemon poured over plenty of ice.

Some pubs now sell apple juice, a splendid drink to be enjoyed as it comes, lightly chilled and drunk outside on a summer's day.

These are just a few ideas using the non-alcoholic drinks, fruit juices and syrups available in any pub. Have fun in the pub inventing your own drinks and finding your own favourites. You'll find plenty of ideas for non-alcoholic cocktails, party and after-dinner drinks in Part Two of this book.

Don't be afraid to ask for what you want

Never be afraid or embarrassed about ordering something

non-alcoholic in a pub. The landlord won't mind mixing it or you can buy the bottles and mix them in the glass yourself. Be inventive. It's fun watching a drink you've concocted and christened catching on. Pubs aren't just in the business of selling alcohol—there's more profit on mixers and soft drinks and the publican would be quite happy if he sold nothing but gallons of lemonade each day. And—surprise, surprise—there are lots of landlords who don't drink.

Order a decent tipple, make sure it is what you want, take your time, don't feel embarrassed, and do make a fuss of it if you want to.

Non-alcoholic beers, wines and spirits

In the last couple of years there has been a dramatic growth in the number of non-alcoholic beers, wines and spirits, following the enormous success of Barbican, the non-alcoholic lager. Many pubs sell Barbican (the best 'safe' lager I have ever tasted) or their own brands. Don't buy these beers at first, wait at least six months before using them. First get used to not drinking and let others get used to you not drinking. Don't hide behind something that looks like a drink. From the very first day it is essential to say and keep on saying, 'I don't drink'. Using a non-alcoholic beer is hiding from the truth. If you truly want to give up, then give up and say so.

There is no substitute for saying no.

Be prepared for leg-pulling

Watching a non-drinker at the bar for the first time, confronting their friends with their new-found abstinence, is like watching one of those wildlife films when a troop of ants discover a dead insect in their path. Like the ants, the pals swarm all over the helpless body, questioning, probing and above all trying to devour the poor creature!

It isn't easy to stop drinking and it doesn't help when stupid friends question the wisdom of giving up. Or start wafting large vodkas or glasses of beer in the face of the convert. But they will.

When you give up drinking be prepared for the reaction you will get in the pub. At first no one will believe you, then they will try enticing you into drinking with gifts of wine and beer laid out invitingly along the bar and finally a lot of people will ignore you. True friends will quickly realise your sincerity and stop behaving like this, but drinking pals will pester you for weeks before finally deserting you.

Some friends, even those behind the bar, will not be able to resist poking fun at you. This is only understandable. To them you are a big drinker and familiar sight in the bar—indeed, many people may never have seen you without a glass of the hard stuff in your hand. They see you as the confirmed drinker and will laugh when you say you have given up. But pretty soon, when they see you are serious, all that will stop.

Bars are places to drink in and so it is only natural at first to feel a bit left out when all around everybody else is drinking. But look again. Not everyone is on the hard stuff; it isn't compulsory.

Coping with the first visit

Gordon is a 30-year-old journalist. He became a heavy drinker through his job. Late nights and odd social hours led to more and more time being spent in the pub. He has now given up drinking completely by following the guidelines in this book, using planning, common sense and will-power to beat the bottle. But when he started two years ago he had no idea. He still remembers his first naive trip to the pub as a fledgeling teetotaller.

It was agony. He just stood at the bar feeling lost and embarrassed. It was as if he were naked. All around him people seemed to be swigging, gulping, shouting, smoking, laughing and generally having a wonderful time and standing slap bang in

17

the middle of them was Gordon, Mr. Orange Juice. His friends, good friends, were with him but Gordon was alone. He could join them by ordering a drink.

This is a crisis that will face you. Think positive. Take a deep breath, clear away the cobwebs and think. Think why you have decided to give up drinking. Think how you will feel in the morning. Think of the good of not drinking and then think of the bad if you fail, and then say no and keep saying no. Remember, the first no is the hardest and then it is easier and easier. Never forget that.

On your first visit to the pub it is a good idea to go late. Aim to arrive with no more than an hour to go of the evening session. This cuts out the major problem—time. Without practice an hour is just about right, not too long and not too short.

Always emphasize to yourself the positive side of giving up. Think of the loss of weight, the healthier body, the greater energy, better sleep and increased peace of mind. Give your friends positive reasons to support you; for instance, if you drive sometimes, offer to do the driving—but not *all* the time. Don't allow yourself to be used. Just because you don't drink anymore you're not a doormat.

Straight away say 'I don't drink'

In the pub tell your friends immediately 'I don't drink'. Be honest and forthright and use the same sentence, 'I don't drink', each time. It's bold and to the point. Get used to saying it. Involve your friends and tell them why. Remember you don't have to tell them everything, decide for yourself how much people should know. Give others the chance to join in your battle and you will be amazed how much they jump at the opportunity to help with love and support.

Never hide away or be ashamed of not drinking. Learn to be proud of it.

18

Should you buy a round?

It is common practice in British pubs to buy rounds of drinks, that is buying a drink for everyone and then letting the others buy one back until everyone has bought everyone else a drink. Buying rounds of drinks is banned in British advertising because it is thought to encourage excessive drinking. I don't know if it does but I recommend all non-drinkers to stand their round unless it is a huge one. Paying out £10 and then getting 15 soft drinks back isn't much fun but, with small rounds of two or three people, it's all right. Financially it will be a little more costly to buy a round instead of three soft drinks but it is the socializing, the joining in, that counts more than the cost. It is especially important not to feel isolated by not drinking, particularly as there is no need.

In general non-drinkers go to the pub a lot less than drinkers and so plenty of money is saved even with buying the odd expensive round.

More women are drinking in pubs

Once only groups of men were found drinking in pubs. Women only went in with a husband or boyfriend. Some bars were for men only. Now young women are becoming pub regulars.

Jean and Barbara began drinking when they were both 16, buying bottles from supermarkets and off-licences. At 18 they began visiting the pub every evening except Saturday and Sunday when they went to a local wine bar. Jean worked in a boutique and Barbara in a record store and after paying mum for their keep they each had between £50 and £60 a week to spend on clothes and drink. Neither of them had any reservations about drinking in a pub and they would down five or six glasses of white wine and soda an evening. Often they would try to match their male friends drink for drink but always found themselves drunk first.

Like many men have done before them, Jean and Barbara

began to drift into a pattern of heavy drinking. This drifting into bad drinking used to be confined to males but with the breakdown of the taboo on women in pubs more and more young women are going the way of the men, paying a heavy price for their emancipation.

At weekends the couple would carry on drinking late into the night at friends' flats or at parties. They would get drunk every night, often turning up late and ill for work and spending all their spare cash on alcohol. They began drinking at lunchtimes, meeting at the High Street pub and having two or three glasses of wine.

Then one night at a party they accepted a lift from a total stranger and he told them the car he was driving was stolen. This really shook them up and they decided to stop drinking.

As soon as they quit they realized they had a big problem and each had been pushing the other into drinking because they thought it was the 'modern' thing to do. They had money, good jobs and no cares and they wasted their time in the pub. They treated it as a sort of youth club with alcohol and they copied their male friends, drinking hard and thinking being drunk was a laugh—only it wasn't.

Barbara and Jean used each other to say no to alcohol. First they agreed that they had quit. Then they told their friends. They refused to join in the heavy drinking, choosing orange juice and mineral water instead. They cut their visits to the pub to twice a week and then only for an hour. Both took up other interests: Barbara went to dance classes and Jean took up photography, and they widened their circle of friends. They soon discovered that not all 18-year-olds were in the pub every night. With the money they saved they went on holiday and Jean bought a scooter. Both of them realized that life at 18 and sober was great—and they haven't touched a drop of alcohol since that fateful car ride.

English licensing laws

The English licensing laws, a system of sessions, and licensing hours like them, do more to create problem drinkers than any amount of advertising, whether or not it shows people buying rounds. The English pub law is designed to stop overdrinking. It does just the opposite.

The sessions system means drinkers never have to say no. They just keep on drinking, often having more than they should because the hours are rationed, until the landlord comes along and calls 'Time'. The conscious decision by the drinker to say no, to make up their mind that they have had enough, is never made. They continue until the decision is made for them. How often, especially in an evening session, do people go home before the end? Not very often.

If there were no licensing sessions English pub drinkers would have to decide when to stop. They would have to take stock of themselves as they drank. At first some people would drink until they fell over, but after a short while they would learn to call 'Time' on themselves. At present the average pub drinker, subject to sessions, is like a child with the landlord as a sort of father figure, telling them when to stop. It is this decisiveness, so lacking in the English pub system at the moment, that is the cornerstone of giving up drinking.

Saying no to alcohol is an adult decision. To go into a bar and dictate the pace is to take hold of your life. To go into a bar and fail to say no when you want to is to let life take hold of you.

Life without drink is easy, easier for some than life with it. Alcohol doesn't affect our lives in any positive way. Everyone can get by without it if they want to.

The pub is a place of fun. A place to meet old friends and make new ones. It is also a place for non-drinkers to show off, show off their new-found will-power, maturity and determination. Go ahead and enjoy it!

4

Drinking at Home

Drinking at home is increasing, especially among women, and it brings with it some special problems, particularly if you live alone or are drinking in secret when family or friends are out. It is entirely up to you to stop it. You have to say no to yourself.

Edna is a 52-year-old middle-class woman living in a detached house in a smart suburb of London. Two years ago she began drinking heavily, up to a bottle of white wine each afternoon and several large gins in the evening. She was regularly drunk. What had changed this happy-go-lucky woman into a person with a drink problem? She had a lovely house, plenty of money, three nice children and a very successful husband. What had happened two years ago to start it all off?

It was then that her youngest son left home for university. With another son abroad, her daughter married, and her husband busy with his career, Edna felt alone. She felt that everything she had lived for, everything that had seemed to give purpose to her life, had gone. She discovered that she didn't really have any close friends. Her neighbours were mere acquaintances. All she seemed to have was an abundance of spare time. She questioned if it was all worth it: what was the point of it all? She felt lonely and sad, and to comfort herself she began drinking.

At first it was just a glass of sherry each afternoon, then two and three. The sherry began to give her headaches so she swopped to white wine—it was better for her figure. In the evenings she would share a few gins with her husband. At night she slept well but often woke very early and found it difficult to go back to sleep.

She knew she was drinking too much and began hiding the empties, taking them to the local dump so they wouldn't mount up in the dustbin and serve as a guilty reminder of how much she was consuming. Occasionally her husband, noticing she was slightly slurred in the early evening, would question her about her drinking but she was alway able to assure him everything was under control and he had no reason to worry. She became a good liar.

Then one day Edna fell asleep in the armchair, forgetting she had turned the iron on. When she woke the dining room was full of smoke, a pile of clothes were scorched and the walls were covered in a sooty grime. It was then that she admitted to herself that she had to stop drinking.

Edna's is a common experience among middle-aged women which results in problem drinking in the home. A chapter of their life, as a mother, provider and protector, is over and they question themselves. The answer is to start a new chapter—not get drunk.

The first thing to do is say to yourself, 'I don't drink', and keep on saying it. Then tell your partner and all your friends. At first they'll think you are joking but be patient with them, they will soon believe you. Try to break the news of your not drinking on your terms. Invite your friends and family around for a small drinks evening and then let them know quite casually that you have given up. By announcing it at home, on your territory you are in command of the situation and can feel comfortable—you are in charge.

Don't be frightened of what others may think, they probably won't think anything of it and if you have had a serious drink problem they will all be relieved and happy for you.

Saying you have given up drinking is a marvellous thing to do; never forget that.

When your children leave home and you are left alone all day, perhaps for the first time in years, it is only natural to look back over your life and wonder if the sacrifices of bringing up a family were worth it. Well of course they were; but now that phase of life is over. Don't see it as the end of life but as the start of a fresh and exciting new era—the chance to begin all over again.

Go out and make new friends, join clubs and societies, play some sport or go back to school. Why not try starting a new career or, if you had a career before the children, why not start it up again? If employment is impossible, charity work certainly isn't. Organizations are crying out for help. Contact your local social services department—they will gladly put you in touch with charities.

There's plenty to do instead of sitting at home like a vegetable feeling sorry for yourself and turning to the bottle.

Break the pattern

Drinking at home normally falls into a pattern, buying the same drink from the same shop, drinking it at the same time, hiding the empties in the same place and feeling very guilty about the whole thing.

The first thing to do is break the pattern. Say 'I'm not going to buy any drink'. Change your shop and choose another that doesn't sell liquor. Try and shop at a different time from what you usually do. Buy your groceries in the morning when your resolve is strongest and get everything that you need in the one go. Never go back later if you have forgotten something—it is just another chance to shop for alcohol.

To take the pressure off the afternoons arrange to go and see someone—if possible make dates to meet people you would absolutely hate to see you drunk. This acts as a break to any desire you may have to go on a binge. If you don't know anyone get out of the house and go for a long walk in a very public place like a nice park, or go and sit in the library.

Breaking the pattern of shopping and drinking makes it easier to say no because you are doing something at times when you would otherwise be getting drunk. Very quickly the desire for alcohol will go and you will be able to walk past an off-licence as if it were a paint store.

By using these tips Edna was able to break the mould. She took on a part-time job, working for the local hospital's visitors group, began piano lessons she had stopped when she got married. She made a lot of new friends and started enjoying her new life.

She learned how to say no to alcohol and discovered the joy of not drinking.

The morning sherry parties

When one person or more is a problem drinker this can lead to heavy drinking among friends and neighbours.

Pat is 26, married with two children, and lives on a housing estate in a new town. She began drinking heavily but has now stopped completely.

She and a group of other young mothers began organizing coffee mornings, meeting at each other's houses to play records and talk. Soon the coffee was being replaced by sherry and the meetings increased from once a week to every day. At first Pat was reluctant to drink but with the others doing it she joined in and was soon pushing the pace. Often the whole group would be the worse for drink, with Pat egging them on. She was drinking more and more and encouraging the others to join her.

Pat realized alcohol was getting a hold over her and decided to stop.

In this situation the group were reinforcing each other's bad drinking habits. Pat only started because she didn't want to feel the odd one out.

With this sort of drinking it is essential to break away from the drinking environment. Pat cancelled the sherry mornings at her home and refused to go when invited to the other's houses, telling them why and that she had given up drinking. At first she felt lonely and out of it but she quickly discovered that most of the people in the group were not real friends, just drinking partners. A few were more than that and with these she remained close, but the others have drifted away. When she stopped drinking she realized their company was not the fun she thought it was.

Pat moved into a new circle of mothers and soon discovered how nice it was being sober in the morning. She really began to enjoy herself. Pat has said no to alcohol and she doesn't miss it a bit.

Don't be tempted to go along with something just because everyone else is doing it. At first you will feel left out because you have made alcohol the centre of your life and those around you will be drinkers. Very quickly all this will change and you will look back on those drinking days and see them as a bad experience you are more than happy to put behind you.

The career woman

More and more women are rejecting the traditional role of the submissive housewife stuck at home with the washing and ironing and are opting for a career. But many women try to combine the two, swapping their executive desks for a dustpan and brush when they come home in the evening. This leads to a lot of stress and they turn to alcohol to cope.

Others feel that in order to compete in a man's world they have to be like the men and that means drinking in pubs and clubs, going to bars at lunchtime and drinking with the boys after work. It is an established fact that women's tolerance to alcohol is considerably lower than men's, and being one of the lads can even prove fatal.

When problem drinking occurs because of this or a person becomes unhappy with their drinking and wants to stop before it becomes a problem they must overcome the natural desire to blend in with the crowd. Saying no is learning to become an individual—and that's a very important quality if you want to go right to the top of your profession.

Television and newspapers portray women executives as supertough bitches and that stereotyped image has caught on. As a result some women in top jobs may feel they have lost their femininity in the race for success and may turn to alcohol to ease this loss, unwinding at home in the evening with a bottle.

Women who do this convince themselves that the alcohol is acting as a sort of medicine helping them overcome the stresses of the day. Women who regularly drink at home after work sometimes invent aches and pains, and swear they are drinking for the benefit of their health.

Drinking does no help stress or banish genuine illnesses. The body is well able to cope with everyday tensions and aches without being tranquillized by alcoholic drink. If you are seriously mentally fatigued you need a doctor, not a cocktail cabinet. A good way to unwind is to develop a genuine hobby which takes your mind off work and drinking. Exercise is also excellent because it builds up a strong and confident body—and that gives you a strong and confident mind.

Anna is 36, married with a baby, and head of a major department in a successful firm in the North of England. After her promotion to head of department her life changed. She found the job a lot more taxing, she had to discipline people she had formerly worked alongside, she was getting home later and still making the family meal and getting up a 6 a.m. every day to feed the baby. She also began bringing work home at weekends.

Soon after the promotion she began fixing herself a drink each evening while the tea was cooking. Then she began fixing herself a couple of drinks. This quickly led to drinking throughout the entire evening. She justified this by saying the alcohol helped her relax and get a good night's sleep before waking up early to feed the baby.

Her drinking increased until, she calculated, she was spending her entire salary increase from the promotion on alcohol. Her executive position meant she was working more for less pay and doing herself damage at the same time. So Anna stopped drinking.

Her problem was she was trying to do too much. You can't run a family, look after a baby and hold down an important job. Work, family and the home have to be reorganized.

Anna, who already had someone to look after the baby

during the day, got a neighbour in to help with the housework. She made her husband prepare the evening meal and pick up the baby, and she stopped bringing work home at weekends. To recharge her batteries she took up exercise and also joined an evening class so that she had something to take her mind off work and the home.

She has cut out lunchtime drinks with fellow managers, choosing only mineral water if she goes to a bar. At first her male colleagues thought she was being wet and tried to talk her into drinking but now they accept the situation without question. Nobody thinks any less of her for not drinking.

Anna has learned to say no to herself and to others.

Loneliness drinking

Among both women and men loneliness can lead people into problem drinking at home. If someone lives alone there is nobody to stop them hitting the bottle. A person who would be happy to chat away over a cup of coffee turns to drink when there is no one to talk to. These people drink at all times of the day, often stuck in front of the television.

Just how many loneliness drinkers there are is impossible to say. Their plight is rarely discovered unless they seek help. To the outsider they are just loners who rarely come out of their home, preferring to be on their own. But the drinker is desperate for company.

The answer for people like this lies with themselves perhaps more than any other group. They have to get out of the house and make friends.

As with all who give up drinking, start by saying no, in this case to yourself. Stop buying alcohol by refusing to go in shops where it is sold. Break the pattern of the day by forcing yourself to go out of the house. Set yourself a target like a walk, a bus ride or a visit to the cinema, nothing too hard. Go to the library and ask the librarian about local groups and meeting places, they will know what is going on in the area.

The only way to end the loneliness and beat the bottle is to tell people you exist. Go to them because they will never come to you.

Lillian didn't begin drinking until after her retirement. For 30 years she was an assistant manageress in the women's section of a prestigious department store. A spinster, she found living alone on her pension a frightening experience. She had never got to know her neighbours except to nod a polite hello. Her sister and family lived 50 miles away and only visited four or five times a year. After an empty first year of retirement Lillian turned to alcohol to brighten up her drab days. She began to drink heavily and at 64 she was drinking a bottle of wine a day and several glasses of brandy, paid for out of her generous company pension. She would often go to bed drunk at 7 or 8 p.m.

She decided to quit drinking following a scare. A cautious woman, her nightly routine had always been to check her fire every night before going to bed because she had a horror of leaving it on all night. This night she got so drunk she fell asleep in her chair and woke to find the fire burning away, both bars blazing. That was it. She poured the remains of her brandy bottle down the sink and vowed never to drink again.

Lillian phoned the local reference library and asked them for a list of clubs in her area. She found there were several that met in the afternoons and, choosing the one she thought she would like most, she went along. It was the start of her new life. She quickly made friends and now finds her sober retirement filled with happiness.

Not drinking in a drinking family

It can seem a lot more difficult to say no at home when the rest of the family are sensible drinkers and like to have alcohol in the house. It seems hard but it isn't. Not drinking is a state of mind and if you don't stop that's up to you. Blaming the rest of the family is just an excuse for your shortcomings.

In this situation take command and prepare the ground. You are allowed to give yourself as much help as you can. Always have lots of soft drinks in the house so as not to feel left out when people are drinking. When others are having a celebration drink mix yourself an exciting non-alcoholic cocktail. They're having a treat so have one yourself. You'll find plenty of ideas in Part Two. Don't overdo the exotic concoctions, that way they are more special when it comes to the big occasions. Keep a good selection of fresh fruits, mixers and syrups to hand—the day you run out, that's the day someone will crack open a bottle of champagne and you'll feel left out.

Don't try to force the rest of the family into not drinking (but do talk to them about it if there is cause for concern about their consumption); if you bully them they will only resent it and may even try to break your resolve to stop.

In a short time your interest in alcohol will go completely and you will ignore other people's drinking without another thought.

Saying no to yourself

Saying no to yourself when there is nobody to chide you, or make you feel guilty or, just as important, praise you, is the ultimate test. It is just you, will-power and conscience. But all non-drinkers have to say no to themselves before they can say no to others; the man in the bar, the woman at the party, the executive at a business lunch, each has said no to themselves before saying it out loud.

Everyone does better with praise and encouragement. If you are alone then you will have to give yourself a pat on the back. Why not put away the money normally spent on drink and reward yourself with a lovely present, something special like a new dress or a bike, perhaps a set of golf clubs or a video.

But most of all make use of your new-found confidence and good looks to go out and make friends. There are plenty of people just waiting to meet you.

5

The party

Like the pub, all it takes to enjoy a party is to be in command and all that takes is a little bit of planning.

Dave is 45 and had been drinking for 25 years before he gave it up. Soon after he went on the wagon he was invited to a friend's birthday party. Armed with a bottle of lemonade he set off.

His visit to the party was undertaken without any planning at all. He just wandered along. It was a nightmare, a high-voltage shock to his delicate alcohol-free system. Yet it could have been great fun if he had gone about it the right way.

He walked into a room full of swirling, shouting people, a room thick with smoke and music and alcohol. A good party in full swing has an atmosphere you can lean up against—and this was a great party! In dark corners, eyes and teeth flashed and the kitchen was awash with spilled beer, paper cups and drunks.

Walking into a party featuring an Aladdin's cave of liquor when you've just decided to give up drinking is a tough test of any new teetotaller's resolve. This party was just such an Aladdin's cave. Here, then, was Dave, standing in a kitchen which resembled a bonded warehouse, where every conceivable type of wine, beer and spirit could be had. Caught unprepared, Dave fell into the silly trap of thinking he couldn't join in unless he had a drink in his hand. Like one of Pavlov's dogs, he had over the years trained himself to associate alcohol with fun until he believed alcohol *was* fun. Take away the drinks, take away the laughs. Of course this is completely wrong.

In learning to say no, going to parties and not drinking, Dave has discovered that he can easily do without alcohol and still have a good time. By going without and finding it fun, Dave has de-programmed himself. This is what you have to do.

Bring your own supplies

Going to a party isn't like popping into a bar. There's no guarantee there will be any non-alcoholic drink, so you have to take your own, and plenty of it—or be stuck with drinking water all night.

I have been to too many parties where there have been no soft drinks at all or I've been told they are for mixing with alcohol only. This is in spite of the fact that many people were driving. On these occasions I've found myself wandering around sharing my rations with the most needy cases. No decent host or hostess should organize a party without providing plenty of mixers and fruit juices—not just to be mixed with the spirits. There should be a cocktail cabinet full of soft drinks.

If it is a large disorganized party hide a bottle, say, in the oven or a cupboard; if it is a more civilized occasion ask the host to look after some and whatever sort of party it is always keep a spare or two in the car.

It is when supplies of lemonade are low that everybody in the world decides they've had enough alcohol and goes on to the soft drinks. A couple of bottles of lemonade are soon polished off by half-a-dozen thirsty mouths.

Try to keep the drink cool, there's nothing worse than warm sticky fizz, and take plenty more than you need. If it's a bottle party don't just take along your own soft drinks; that's mean, stingy and just plain selfish. The host is providing their home for the party, music, people and quite often food, so give them a bottle of wine as a thank you. People would soon get fed up and the party invitations would start to dry up if all they ever saw from you were bottles of minerals or cordials.

Timing is important

Dave's first party seemed to last years. He had fallen victim to the old enemy of the new non-drinker, time. His arrival at the party had been far too early and he paid for the mistake. It is important to plan how long you want to stay and to time the entrance right. Two or three hours is long enough the first couple of times and it is better to arrive late and leave when the others do, rather than get there first and leave just as everyone is beginning to enjoy themselves. Leaving early makes you feel terribly left out and miserable.

Advantages for the unattached

If you're single, arriving late and staying fresh has a big advantage. It is a lot easier to find a partner when you are stone cold sober, and that goes for both men and women. There's no reason these days why women as well as men can't ask a person to dance and a request coming from a lively, sensible, sober person is far more likely to get a positive response.

People trust you when you are sober, especially driving. This means that, at the end of a party, just when the drink-soaked romantics are making their moves, you can move in and whisk the darling of your dreams off their feet and into your arms. Being able to use the car both legally and sensibly is a big plus. And again, most people would rather be chatted up by someone who is sober and nice than someone plainly the worse for wear.

So far from being a damper, not drinking at a party has some very positive advantages.

Being sober at the end of a party also means you needn't end up sleeping on the floor, waking up to the sight of empty beer cans and bottles strewn all over the place and feeling as if you had been run over by a steamroller in the early hours of the morning. Or waking to hear the thunderous roar of the dawn chorus and taking ten panic-stricken minutes to discover you have slept the last four hours upside down in the back of a car. Or, perhaps worst of all, waking up to find you are in bed with someone else, someone you don't want to be with, and with your sweetheart's picture poking out of the inside pocket of your coat hanging on the end of the bed and not knowing what's worse, the guilt, the shame . . . or the headache.

Staying sober cuts out all this. When you wake up in the morning you'll be where you want to be and feel good for it.

Say only what you want to say

It is at parties that people will manipulate you into a corner and drill you for hours on why you have given up drinking. They are spurred on by a sort of morbid curiosity—they think that if they push just a little bit further they will reveal some naughty secret. They will discover, perhaps, that when you are drunk you steal bicycles and pass out on the way home. They hope that you will suddenly crack, fall down prostrate in front of the fridge and admit everything.

When this happens tell them that you don't drink because you have given it up and feel a lot better for it. When they persist you can either continue to stress the benefits of not drinking or ignore them. Tell them just what you want to tell them. There is no reason on earth why you should say anything more, unless of course you want to. Going sober doesn't mean you have to throw open the doors of your soul to any nosey parker who happens to feel smugly curious. Giving up drinking is a brave, honest thing to do for whatever reason. It is enough just to say 'I don't drink'. You don't have to say anything more because you have said it all.

Drinking and nerves

Some people get very nervous before going to a party. They want to look their best, to feel attractive, they want to have a laugh and appear witty and confident. They see the party as a trial with themselves under scrutiny and, most important, they can come away from a party feeling they have failed. To combat this and give themselves an edge they drink before it starts; while others are going to the party to get drunk they get drunk to go to the party. Once you start you never stop and this drinking to boost your self-esteem seeps into other areas of your life. In the end you are drinking just to have the confidence to go to the shops.

And the sad part is it doesn't work. Nobody thinks you are funnier, smarter, more articulate. They just think you are drunk.

Margaret was a pretty 40-year-old with a lovely figure, a quick mind and a good sense of humour. At small dinner parties she was the centre of attention but in large crowds she felt swamped. Whenever she went to a party she hated it. Then one day she got very drunk and everyone overlooked it, and said it was funny. This, thought Maggie, was the answer and she began drinking before every party. Then she began drinking heavily hours before each party, getting more and more drunk each time. She began drinking for confidence, but now the drinking was undermining her confidence. She had become another victim of alcohol's vicious circle.

The answer was to break the cycle, to say no to alcohol. Only then would she be able to cope.

Margaret was frightened of large party crowds and so she hid behind drink, using it as a shield to protect her. Why did she hate those parties? In a crowded room she felt conspicuous and lonely. She was shy about joining in conversations, especially if she didn't know anyone and would hover around the perimeter of a group too scared to open her mouth. If anyone drew her into the conversation she would get flustered and freeze up. So she turned to alcohol to melt the ice and oil her tongue. She would drink half a bottle of wine before turning up and then several glasses very quickly after she arrived. When most people were into their second glass she was drunk. Her protecting shield of alcohol only made her more isolated. So she became more unhappy and drank more. She was drinking to have a good time at parties and all she had to do was stop drinking and believe in herself.

One day her husband refused to take her to a party because she had got too drunk beforehand and it was then she decided her drinking had to stop. She had to have the courage to find out for herself that not drinking was not an impossible nightmare but the key to happiness.

At the first couple of sober parties she felt scared but also proud of herself. She realized that not drinking was a virtue, something to show off and for the first time she understood how stupid her drinking had been. Her whole attitude had changed —partly because she felt more relaxed and confident—but also because of the reactions of other people. They saw the new woman and they liked what they saw. The centre of attention at a small dinner party, she could now hold her own in a large gathering.

She was still sometimes overcome with shyness and was always nervous before a party, but she didn't turn to the bottle for comfort. Instead she learnt not to be afraid of these feelings but to accept and get over them.

It is important to remember that everyone feels nervous at times, not just you. In a room of strangers, everybody is shy.

As soon as she stopped drinking Margaret made no secret of it. In order to give up you can't pretend. If Margaret had appeared to be still drinking she would have had nothing to be proud of and her resolve wouldn't have lasted five minutes.

Don't lie

Never lie about not drinking, never make excuses. Not drinking is nothing to be ashamed of, don't ever forget that, and lying always leads to needless complications. And if you lie to others you will end up lying to yourself.

Drink doesn't help

Whenever I went to a party it always took me a couple of hours before I braved the dance floor. These couple of hours were needed to loosen up and 'get in the mood'. Getting in the mood meant getting drunk. After a few stiffeners I was ready to go out on the floor and wow them and for years this is exactly what I thought I was doing. It was only after I gave up drinking that I realized my dancing technique resembled a cross between Mick Jagger and Long John Silver on a trampoline. My dancing was terrible and I was getting up Dutch courage to perform it, not realizing the rest of the party needed Dutch courage to watch it. Now I enjoy dancing and so do my partners; I'm a great deal better since I gave those 'looseners' a miss. There is nothing that is truly done better after a few drinks—whatever we may think.

Like the example of Dave, I was lost at my first party and spent the whole time being a wallflower. While most people danced, smooched and kissed, I cuddled up with a warm cup of cola. I was miserable and it was my own fault. I have no excuses. Parties are just as good fun, just as good a laugh, better in fact, when you're sober.

A party without alcohol is not the end of the world. A party isn't just drinking—it's music, food, conversation, dancing, romance and fun. Make the most of it and enjoy yourself—without alcohol.

6

The restaurant

Wine, the fermented juice of the grape, has been drunk with food for at least 3000 years—and so has water. Just like wine, natural mineral water aids the digestion, cleans the palate and complements a good meal. Today, all good restaurants stock a range of bottled waters, of both the still and the fizzy kind.

When you have given up drinking a restaurant can seem a daunting place. There is such a snobbishness attached to dining out, especially choosing the wine, that non-drinkers could be forgiven for baulking at the prospect and settling for a hamburger.

Wine is nothing to be afraid of and, with a little planning, avoiding it and other alcohol in a restaurant is quite easy.

The key, as always with not drinking, is to take command of the situation and not let the situation take command of you. Wine waiters always presume that everyone at the table is drinking. The first thing to do is let them know you are not.

Right from the start
say you're not drinking

The first time Tim went into a restaurant after giving up drinking he was embarrassed about looking out of place. To counter this he ordered a full bottle of wine between two, watched the waiter fill both glasses and half-way through the meal swapped the glasses over so it looked as if he was drinking. No sooner had he done this than the waiter sidled over and gave his glass a top up. He felt stupid. Tim had fallen into the trap of pretending he was drinking. Never be ashamed of not drinking.

Because he had started the deception he had to finish it and each time the waiters weren't looking he kept switching the glasses over. It would have made television magician Paul Daniels proud.

By the end of the evening Tim's girlfriend, in order to keep up the pretence, had drunk an entire bottle of wine and almost had to be scraped off the restaurant floor and into his car.

Tim's problem was that he was intimidated by the wine waiter. He pretended for the sake of conformity, thinking it very unsophisticated not to drink with a meal.

Never lie about not drinking. This is the golden rule.

Tim should have taken command right from the start and not allowed the situation to develop. Confront the problem and the problem will go away, hide from it and it will be there all the time, dominating and ruining the day.

Tim should have said immediately: 'I don't drink'.

Don't be scared of the wine waiter

Right at the beginning of your meal explain to the waiter that you do not drink and will be taking a soft drink during the meal. This does not always sink in and if you are ordering food you may be offered the first sip of wine to taste. If this happens, and it often does, don't make a fuss, simply pass the glass to your nearest companion and say something like: 'Here, your taste buds are pretty sharp, taste this'; or 'You know a thing or two about wine, after you'. After the tasting quietly remind the waiter that you are not drinking wine.

Sometimes the waiter without thinking and before anyone has noticed pours everyone a glass of wine. If this happens leave yours and ignore it until the end of the meal, when you can offer it around if anyone has room for an extra glass.

If, during the meal, the waiter comes to top up everyone's glass simply put the palm of your hand over your glass and the waiter will miss the glass out.

Order buckets of water and share it around

Lots of people think that drinking water instead of wine with a meal is boring. They're wrong. Naturally fizzy mineral water is as exhilarating and refreshing as any glass of Chablis or Beaujolais. In many respects sparkling water is much better, leaving the mouth fresh and the head clear.

The trick with mineral water is in the presentation. It should be drunk with panache, with style. The glass should be big and full of ice, with a huge wedge of lemon lying on top and the water should always be poured over this mountain of lemon and ice. It should then be slooshed around the mouth and swallowed hard.

Don't be mean with the water, order it for everyone and drink buckets of it with the meal. The great thing about water, unlike, say, orange juice, is that it doesn't leave a taste in the mouth. The full flavour of the meal can be enjoyed unhindered.

For most people eating out is a special occasion and drinking a couple of glasses of cola with a meal would spoil it. The nice thing about mineral water, particularly the lovely fizzy ones, is that they are different and that bit more special than everyday soft drinks—and they don't look out of place on the dining table.

The health-conscious businessman or businesswoman has long preferred Perrier water as the fashionable alternative to alcohol. Those watching their weight will be pleased to know that mineral waters contain no calories.

When eating out as a couple, where one drinks and the other does not, don't forget that restaurants, if they are the least bit good, serve half-bottles of wine. If there are no half-bottles on the wine list, ask. If the restaurant does not sell half-bottles I would leave, explaining why. It is a good bet that if they can't be bothered with half-bottles they can't be bothered with the rest of the operation, including the food.

The business lunch

Coping with the wine waiter is easier when those around you know you do not drink. It is a little bit harder when the occasion

is a business lunch. At a working meal first impressions are
important and the pressure is on to conform and keep up with
others in the drinking.

Once more the answer is to take command. Explain the
situation as soon as it is possible to do so. Be decisive. Clear the
air straight away. There is nothing worse than clamming up and
half talking to people when all the time your mind is building up
to the moment when you will be asked what wine you want with
the meal. Say 'I don't drink', and then quietly and confidently
steer the conversation on to a different subject. If you dwell too
long on not drinking you blow the whole thing up and people
begin to feel uncomfortable. Remember, when two or more
people meet for the first time everyone, not just you, is feeling a
little nervous and unsure of themselves. Take advantage of this
to gain control.

Feel proud of not drinking and you will find others sense your
pride and a little of that will rub off on them, creating a good
impression.

Alcohol in cooking

When you cook with alcohol it all evaporates leaving the dish
with just the flavour of the drink. So a meal of entrecôte steak in
red wine sauce is non-alcoholic and perfectly safe to eat. If
alcohol is poured on to a dish after cooking or there is no
cooking involved, such as pineapple and kirsch then, because
the alcohol has not evaporated, the meal is alcoholic.

If you are in doubt about a meal or you don't like the idea of
alcohol-based sauces, however they are cooked, then leave well
alone. 'If in doubt leave it out' is a good motto to remember.

After dinner

Part Two lists some excellent non-alcoholic after-dinner cocktails you can make up. But if you've nothing else but coffee
available don't worry: good, strong, fresh ground coffee
finishes off a meal as well as any other drink.

Far from being a big bore, not drinking can really improve the enjoyment of a meal. Without wine the full subtleties of the flavour of the food can be tasted. Water is better for the health and the waistline and keeps a clear head for important business decisions and for driving home.

7
Sex

Paul should have learnt his lesson the first time it happened. He was standing in a bar eyeing up a delicious blonde girl sitting at a table a few feet away. He smiled, she smiled, he had a beer. Paul looked again, he smiled, she smiled, he had another drink. And so it went on for more than an hour.

At last he decided, several beers later, that it was the right time to make his move. 'I'll just nip out and smarten up', he thought. He slipped out of the bar and into the cloakroom, combed his hair, checked his looks in the mirror, took a deep breath and marched manfully back into the lounge. She was gone. While he had taken his time someone had taken the girl. A while later he saw her in the next room, dancing in another man's arms. He smiled, she just shrugged her shoulders, he ordered another drink.

You would have thought Paul would have learnt his lesson from an experience like that, wouldn't you? Not at all. He must have repeated that scene a hundred times. Beer always came first and, too often, last as well.

The James Bond syndrome

In the love game the heavy-drinking man always has that glass or two before approaching anyone. He does it for two reasons: first, to gain a mild stimulus and overcome any shyness; second, because he has an image of drink as being macho. These two reasons coalesce and it is not really possible to pull them apart. They are both equal in his thinking, acting independently and together at the same time.

This macho image of drinking among men is pretty universal. Paul wouldn't have felt comfortable propositioning someone without a drink in his hand. He thought that being slightly tipsy was roguish, the sort of characters David Niven and Roger Moore play rolled into one—a bit of a card but a demon in bed. Looking back he blushes at how ridiculous he was, half-cut and incapable of driving, thinking he reminded people of James Bond.

But when Paul eventually gave up drinking he found, to his surprise, that he was a lot more attractive without it. He didn't need alcohol to talk to people, it didn't make him funnier or nicer. This revelation boosted his confidence and really helped him cut out drink—because he could see life was better without it.

Port and lemon for girls, whisky for men

Paul had an image of drinking, and drinks themselves have an image. Vermouth, gin and anything but tonic, half-pints of lager and lime, port and lemon, and sweet sherry are all women's drinks. Men drink gin and tonic, dark rum, strong dry cider, lager and whisky.

In the same way, men think soft drinks are for girls and when a man gives up drinking he has to overcome this prejudice. Women will not laugh at you for drinking pineapple juice.

And some men don't feel happy unless the woman they are with is drinking alcohol. They feel calmer and more in control if she has had a few drinks. In this way men use drink in their courting ritual: 'Let's have a few drinks and get to know each other.' Never be pressured by a partner into drinking. You can have just as good a time on the soft stuff.

Amanda is single, 25, and began drinking heavily after she split up with her long-term boyfriend. Derek had been her first lover and had lived with her for three years and known her for six. After the break-up Amanda found sex with other boy-friends difficult. She was nervous and shy, despite a very active sexual relationship in the past with her live-in lover. Then one of her new boyfriends suggested she got drunk before they made love. It did the trick and for the first time in ages she felt good about sex. The next time she made love Amanda drank a bottle of wine beforehand. She did it again the following time and the next and the next. She justified what she was doing by saying the drink was like a medicine helping her to relax. Soon she was using alcohol to stay calm whenever she met a new man.

Amanda had developed a drink problem because she associated good, happy, physical relationships with alcohol. She had convinced herself that romance only came in a bottle. She was wrong. All she needed was to unwind and not try so hard. You don't need a drink for that; it's an attitude of mind.

Her earlier flops weren't even failures. She had read in magazines and books about the new era of fast-loving, fulfilled young women, who flitted like sweet-scented butterflies from man to man, and when her own love-making didn't measure up she thought she was a bedroom disaster. She was comparing herself to a world that only exists between the covers of glossy magazines. Hours of wild passion just aren't the norm in most households. But the bottle seemed to help.

Her lovemaking was now relaxed but it was all a blur and the rest of her life was beginning to suffer. She was having hangovers, feeling guilty and above all she wasn't happy. She determined to quit.

After she stopped drinking she once again found sex awkward and clumsy; she was shy and unsure of herself. But this time she didn't hit the bottle. Gradually she learned to relax without alcohol. She stopped trying to make fantastic story-book love and waited, accepting that good sex would come with love and the right person. She chose her partners more carefully and let laughter and romance take the place of drink. And it worked.

Drinking doesn't improve

Drinking cannot turn a person into someone they are not. If you are shy no amount of alcohol will change that. It has to come from within.

Drinking doesn't impress

People cannot stand being romanced by someone who is the worse for drink. It is the world's biggest turn-off.

When I was 18 and in my last year at school my friend quit his A-level studies to become a dye-pot cleaner in a plastics factory (quite why I have never found out). Each morning as I waited for my bus I would see him cycle past to work on a battered second-hand grocer's bike he had bought with his first week's wages.

For months he had had his eye on a dark-haired beauty at the local girl's school but, not having any spare cash, he'd kept his interest down to simply window-shopping. Flushed with his second week's wages he asked her out. She accepted. He was overjoyed. In a fortnight he'd achieved a dramatic change of fortune. I had school, Louis XIV and ox-bow lakes; he had money and a woman.

For their first date he arranged to meet her in town and promptly took her to the pub—he should have taken her to the cinema. They liked each other but were a bit shy and awkward. Instead of talking through this he turned to alcohol to loosen them up. After quite a few drinks she asked him what he did for a living. 'I'm a long-distance lorry driver. Mainly the Eastern Med and the Middle East', he said. The words astonished him. They floated out of the air almost as if an invisible man were standing at the table. But after the initial shock he warmed to his new profession and was soon gleefully telling her tales of exotic Araby, of beautiful Turkish dancers and trips through the wilds of Persia. She was hooked and through his glassy eyes he loved her. The evening was a fantastic success.

To round it off he would get her home in style—by taxi. He was just about to go and phone for one when she asked, surprised, why he didn't have a car. The drink and the warm night had turned his head and in his desire to kiss her he had lost concentration. 'Sorry', he crooned, 'I haven't got my driving licence yet.' The words were out of his drunken head before he could stop them. As they appeared in the hot summer air her love for him melted like a warm chocolate bar.

Drink had made him fashion a glass crown and drink had smashed it into a hundred thousand pieces.

When you take people out for the evening and you don't drink your head is always clear, and that's a fantastic feeling. You never find yourself bragging or showing off because of the alcohol or, like my friend, inventing silly stories. With drink there is the temptation to embellish things, promote yourself or invent interests you don't have. But there is no need for any of that. People like you as you are. It isn't until the drinker gives up their habit that they realize this.

Drink and romance isn't just a mixture that loosens the tongue, it's a cocktail that can make people do the craziest things.

For some months after it opened the local disco was the in place to go. The nearest thing to a West End club, it drew in the crowds, including many of the best-looking men and women, for twenty miles or more. What made this disco different from all the rest was that next to the dance floor was a swimming pool. And it was besides this that one of the most spectacular examples of red-faced drunkenness happened.

After drinking all night in a pub a group of friends decided to go to the disco, mainly to carry on drinking but also to go looking for girls. (In their state they would have done better to go home and sleep it off.) When they arrived their luck was in; there must have been three girls for every man there. True to form, the lads ignored them all and immediately began a session of heavy drinking, propping up the bar and eyeing up all the 'talent'. Half-a-dozen glasses of beer later their lager-soaked thoughts were on sex. As they scanned the dance floor the tallest member of the gang, Alan, a strapping 6ft 4in, looked across the room from his high vantage point and saw the girl of his dreams. Under normal circumstances he might have asked her to dance. But this was no ordinary disco—this place had a swimming pool. To his friends' amazement he suddenly tore off all his clothes and stood by the pool stark naked. The dancers rushed to the opposite side and were watching, giggling, shouting and clapping their encouragement. He saw none of this, just the beautiful girl now a few feet away from him on the other side. He braced himself for a graceful swallow dive into the blue water. But instead of diving straight out in front he decided to dive sideways—and completely missed the pool. His head hit the marble surround and he crumpled into a heap out cold, blood pouring from his forehead. An ambulance was called and amid thunderous cheers he was carried out naked on a stretcher. The next Alan knew he was coming round in the casualty unit of the local hospital. He has never been back to the club.

Alan's was the classic case of someone having a few drinks before chatting someone up and then making a complete fool of himself because he had had those drinks. Drink and sex went straight to his head. But discos and girls are just the same without alcohol. It's a lot more fun being sober. That goes also for women who have a few drinks for the same kind of reason as Alan, the women who drink for confidence.

The belief among drinkers that a few drinks makes them more attractive in the romance stakes is utterly false. Not drinking means not getting into these daft situations. It's lovely to be able to meet someone nice and to take them out, chat to them, drive them home and drink their coffee feeling relaxed and confident. It's great to know you are completely in charge of your emotions and won't suddenly drop down on one knee and propose to someone you've only known four hours—or accept a proposal.

It is actually in bed that drink can do its biggest damage.

We all know stories of passion thwarted by excess of drink and the resultant embarrassment of 'brewer's droop'. Alcohol is a giant sedative, slowing you down, numbing your reactions and making you heavy and tired, blurred at the edges: not the best condition to be in for exciting love-making. Giving up alcohol is a bit like giving up smoking, in that it heightens your awareness and makes you more sensitive. Sex when sober is splendid, and more readily appreciated than when drunk, and you can remember every detail the following morning. Despite the marketing image of drinks (you know the sort of thing— sexy men and women with their sophisticated after-dinner tipples, skiing trendies with their liquored laughter)—alcohol is the last thing you need for a night of romance.

8

No Hangovers

Life without alcohol means no hangovers, no pain. It is a fantastic feeling to know that you are never again going to suffer the hell of a hangover, that both the physical and mental hurt are banished forever.

At first life without drink might not seem that dramatically different. Waking up is still hard work, your mind is still a bit clogged and fuzzy and tiredness fills your bones. But after a couple of weeks the change is dramatic.

The horror of the 'morning after'

I remember as if they were yesterday the dreadful hangovers of my drinking days. I can't imagine how I used to get through them. Morning would come and, as I gradually opened my eyes, the blinding light hitting my brain would bring with it my hangover, a cocktail of consciousness, guilt and pain. I would lie in bed and misery would sweep over me in continuous waves, each wave worse than the one before. After a few minutes I would be saturated in misery, my brain and body soaked.

These hangover mornings were the lowpoints of my life, a hell on earth. They are feelings shared not just by men. More and more women are turning to the bottle.

Carol became a problem drinker in her early twenties. She has now kicked the habit. Her favourite drink is mineral water. But she can still recall her heavy drinking days. The morning after one of her many bouts of heavy drinking, guilt and shame would hang about Carol's head like dark clouds around a bleak and lonely mountain top. From the moment she woke, these feelings, particularly the almost indescribable feeling of deep shame, would be with her. It bore no relation to what she had done the previous night, just getting drunk was enough to make her hang her head.

Often Carol would have no idea what she'd been up to the previous night. Her mind would draw a heavy curtain across her memory, leaving it a total blank. She simply did not know what she'd been doing. The only certainty was that, wherever she had been, she had got drunk. Not remembering didn't make it any easier, either. No, it just added to her feelings of absolute terror. What had she done? Where had she been? Why couldn't she remember? These questions would follow her, nagging at her coat tails.

On these occasions, far too numerous, she would lie in bed in a state of acute depression unable to go on with life. She would give anything, anything to undo the drunkenness of the past few hours. She hated herself to the core. It disgusted her that she had become a drink-soaked wreck.

Half a day later she would go to the pub.

These mornings of purgatory, of confession and hand-wringing did nothing to stop Carol drinking. She would make the odd attempt to cut down, she missed out rounds, tried using more mixers to make the drink go further, but that was it. She still carried on drinking.

After a while the feeling of guilt each morning became a fixture of her life, it was with her even when she hadn't got drunk the night before. Carol was becoming paranoid and those awful physical hangovers were there as well.

Her legs and arms would turn to jelly and she would have to take in great gulps of fresh air before attempting anything more difficult than standing up. She would keep feeling dizzy and be totally incapable of attempting the simplest mental tasks. Hangovers left Carol a complete wreck.

It wasn't until she learned to say no and carry on saying no that she managed to break the cycle of drink – pain – drink and found the joy of not drinking.

Like Carol, I suffered from hangovers and the physical side was always bad. I would wake up with a dreadful headache and often the pain would be so bad I would want to be sick. The light would scorch my eyes and I knew it would be impossible to keep down anything stronger than a cup of weak tea for at least the first two hours. But still through all this I continued to drink and, like Carol, after a while my life settled into a pattern of overindulgence and hangovers. Then one day I woke up and said 'never again' and I haven't touched a drop of drink since and I don't want to. I love not drinking.

You'll feel better without alcohol

After one week of not drinking the change is already noticeable. Your head clears, your body begins to ache less and the mind becomes clearer and sharper. After a couple of weeks your sense of smell and taste returns and food is a lot more enjoyable. That acheing tiredness starts to disappear fast and it is easier to get up in the morning.

Though it is easier to get up, at first it is harder to sleep at night. This is because for years alcohol has been used as a sleeping pill and when it's no longer there the body finds it hard to cope. You lie awake for what seems hours before dozing off. But, luckily this doesn't last long. The insomnia takes about a week to ten days to get over, and when that happens sleep is beautiful. It is so much more relaxing, more restful and peaceful, like the sleep you enjoyed as a child. Since a week after giving up drinking I have never had a sleepless or restless night.

Waking up alcohol-free is a marvellous sensation which, sadly, too many people are missing out on. Even a few drinks a day makes a difference. The concoctions people pour down their throats in the name of adulthood must be having an affect. Drink is a drug and taking a drug for years and years can't be good for us.

Cutting out drink turns mornings from a nightmare to a joy. You wake up to greet each new dawn happy, confident and refreshed. Today, I have no horrors about waking up—an action I used to dread.

Getting up without a hangover is delightful and makes going

to work so very much easier. It is not until you give up and are able to go off to work with a clear head and a happy heart that you realize just how often you staggered out of the house with a headache or a numb brain.

Instead of feeling ill for the best part of the day Carol now gets up and has a bath before going to work, an act that would have led to her drowning four years ago. On buses and trains she reads newspaper and books, instead of staring out of the window clasping her hands and trying not to be ill. She can travel on the rush-hour tube without thoughts of fainting, she even smiles in the mornings.

It takes about a month for the full physical horrors of hangovers to be purged from the system. It is a gradual process and every new day it gets better and better, so don't be put off at the start, there are no miracles, just stick with it and you will find a new person breaking through. It really is worth it.

Drinking hurts the mind

The physical and mental effects of drinking are intertwined and directly affect each other. Drinking brings you down, makes you feel tired and ill—and this affects the mind.

A hangover makes you feel depressed, guilty, anxious, ashamed, nervous and irritable. These lead to a general shutting down of the most important feeling of all—will. The desire to do something, to make changes, is lost in a general haze of feeling unwell and unhappy. It naturally follows that the more hangovers you get, the worse this will be. This general loss of spark and desire is a breeding ground for all sorts of other problems of the mind like depression, anxiety and paranoia. It can lead to horrible feelings of victimization. Why me? is a common question asked by the heavy drinker.

Hangover mornings are always spent in a vacuum without positive feelings and ability. When coupled with physical pain and sickness this is known as 'having the voids'. The desire in these situations is to curl up into a foetal ball and sleep forever, cocooned from the real world. All this worry is alcohol-based. Take away the hangover and you take away the reason for the worry and the anguish.

But at first taking away the reason does not take away the worry. You can compare it with people who have irrational fears, of spiders for example. They know the spider can't really hurt them but that doesn't stop them being afraid. Take away the reason for the drinker's fear, stop drinking, and that doesn't stop them being scared. This is because the residue from all the drinking days is still there. It is hard to accept that it has gone away, rather like the First World War soldiers who, after it was all over, continued to listen out for the whine of the shells. This is a perfectly natural and rational feeling after living with something for a long time. In the beginning it is going to continue to be a bit bad; you're still going to feel a little anxious. But things will improve.

As the horrible body feelings die so the mental ones die also. As the body gets fitter, stronger and more relaxed so the brain gets stronger and is able to cope with more. The combined effect of the mind and body daily growing, gaining power and confidence, is terrific. It is like taking a drug of deliciously sweet, pure goodness.

A few alcohol- and hangover-free months brings you back up to the sort of cleansed and refreshed mind and body you probably last enjoyed as a schoolchild. Years of drink and the body abuse it brings have been overturned. It doesn't take all that long.

It is a state I have enjoyed for more than four years. I could never go back. To do so would be like swapping a rose for a maggot.

9

Talk about it

Only when they get right to the bottom of the slippery slope, when going further down would mean becoming a drunken drop-out, only then do many people ask for help.

Women who are drinking too much are generally very embarrassed to admit it—far more so than men. They hide away drinking in secret, ashamed and guilty. One of the biggest reasons for this is the social stigma attached to women drinkers. While it is great fun, even admirable, for a man to get drunk, a drunken woman is often looked on with loathing and contempt. So women don't own up when they should. Men will also develop a strong drinking pattern before recognizing they should stop. Both men and women continue their bad drinking habits long after they should quit.

But must people suffer so much before crying for help? The answer is no. What is needed is some honest talk.

If you have a friend or loved one who is hurting themselves with alcohol then tell them. It's hard but it has to be faced. Make them square up to their drinking. Don't avoid or ignore it, that's the last thing the big drinker needs.

People who give up often say that for years they drank too much but it wasn't until they stopped that friends started saying, 'Well, we had noticed you drank quite a bit', or 'I thought you used to get drunk quite a lot'. Something should have been said earlier. It would have brought the whole thing out into the open and made them face up to the facts. When no one mentions a drink problem it gives the heavy drinker the chance to lie to themselves. They pretend that there is nothing to worry about, though deep down they know the truth. It must be all in their head, they kid themselves, an exaggeration. After all, nobody else is talking about their drinking so it can't be all that bad—can it?

This is not an excuse for heavy drinkers. They can't throw up their hands and say? 'Nobody told me I had a drink problem'. No, that's all down to the drinker. But if you know somebody who is drinking too much and heading for trouble, speak to them about it.

Talking is the only answer

If you have a problem then talk about it. Go on, dare yourself, people won't be mad or disgusted, you will feel so much better as soon as you share your heavy load.

I learnt to say no to alcohol by talking. I talked to my wife Ruth and then to my friends. There is no other way to give up drinking than talking about the problem and the difficulties you have faced and are facing. Once the thing has been brought out into the open everyone should have their say; everyone should speak out.

Talking makes you face the truth—though in the end you have to face that truth alone, because in the end you have to come to terms with yourself. Nobody can do that for you. But everybody can help.

Once you have reached a decision to stop it is very easy to work out a plan of what to do next. I say a plan, but in those first moments of awakening reality it is more a resolution; just say to yourself 'Well now I know what I face I'm never going to have another drink'. Having said that go out and tell the world. Each time you meet someone go and tell them, so that soon all your friends and family know what you are doing.

People are surprised and cynical when I tell them that giving up, apart from a few hard times at the beginning, is easy. They think I must be glossing over bad bits. But on the whole it *is* very easy. This is because you share the experience with everyone. You talk about it. Giving up something that everyone else appears to enjoy can be very lonely and that loneliness can make it awfully hard—so don't keep it all to yourself.

I talked to anyone and everyone who would listen and there

were plenty eager to hear my story (some perhaps too eager). I told people over and over again and I never tired of hearing my story and showing off my will-power. Today I'm still just as delighted to talk about it.

Talking acts as a therapy. The more you say the easier it becomes and the problems of not drinking just melt away. You realize it isn't the big deal you'd imagined it to be. You can easily handle it.

Talking isn't just good for you; it is very good for your family and friends. They will all find it a tremendous relief to get the problem aired—and feel a great deal better for it.

I was never told off or looked down upon. Instead I was praised and congratulated and this of course made it even easier for me.

So if you have a problem, or just want to stop, or if you know someone in trouble then talk about it. It is only when people start talking that it can all be sorted out.

10

Getting Help from Others

For some people giving up the bottle is too big a battle to fight on their own. If this is your problem, don't get frightened. What you need is expert help. This works for thousands of people who need that little bit of extra support, especially in times of crisis. There is a whole range of organizations and services that deal with drink problems. The following is a list of the main ones found in the UK, similar groups and facilities can be contacted abroad. Study the various types and choose the one that is best for you.

The family doctor

The first person you should go to with a drink problem, your doctor will be able to put you in touch with a whole range of services. Tell your GP what is wrong, don't expect him or her to diagnose your problem without help from you—doctors are not mind-readers. Remember, you can talk to your doctor in confidence, so don't be afraid to speak up.

Alcoholics Anonymous

Alcoholics Anonymous is the most famous of all the help groups. It is a network of self-help groups run for alcoholics by former alcoholics. There are more than 1000 groups in England and Wales. It is open to both women and men and is strictly confidential. It also has two other groups, Al-Ateen and Al-Anon, for children and families of alcoholics. You'll find their address in your local phone book, or your local reference library will be able to give it to you.

Councils on Alcoholism

There are 46 councils in the UK. At each local branch problem drinkers can get help and advice on all aspects of their drinking. Families of heavy drinkers can also get support. Counselling, talking through the problem and trying to find solutions, is normally on a one-to-one basis—just you and them. Like Alcoholics Anonymous, you can find the address of your nearest branch in your local reference library.

Day centres

These are a number of walk-in centres where people can go for help. No appointment is necessary, just turn up and you will be seen. Many go along on a daily basis for therapy and counselling. These centres are one step from residential facilities where problem drinkers are admitted for a course of treatment. Find out if there is a local centre near you by contacting your branch of the Council on Alcoholism or the Social Services department.

These are the four main ways of getting help. Don't hesitate to use them. Contact someone today.

11

The future

I gave up drinking and I'm still in one piece. And I shall go on staying sober forever. Since that first day when I hid away in the cinema to avoid the temptation to go out drinking, I have never again succumbed to the temptations of alcohol.

Never cut yourself off from everything because you don't drink—it's part of the challenge. Let's face it, there would be no point if you gave up drinking only to end up living like a hermit. So go out to pubs and parties, eat in licensed restaurants, join in with everyone but don't drink. And continue going out and have a good time doing it.

Looking back, those first days were a bit difficult, adjusting my attitude, getting used to the idea of never drinking again. It seemed a massive decision, out of all proportion with my life. I was scared. Scared of failure and, crazy as it sounds, scared of success. What would this new life bring to me and, just as important, would I be able to cope? I felt like an explorer about to enter a jungle tunnel; would it lead to a tropical paradise or a tribe of savage headhunters?

I had nothing to fear. I soon realized my decision had been the best one I had ever made.

Once I had determined to stop it was easy and fun. Giving up was enjoyable. I liked being sober. I liked saying, 'I don't drink'. I liked feeling fitter and looking good.

I never think about drinking unless someone remarks on the fact that I don't. I never feel like a drink or get bored because I am not drinking even when I am the only one. I don't avoid alcoholic situations because I am never aware of them. Drinking has gone out of my life and I don't miss it. When you give up, alcohol will quite quickly go from your life and, like me, you will wonder why you didn't give it up years ago.

The future without alcohol is a welcoming thought. It's like settling into your favourite comfy armchair at the end of a long and tiring journey. You can put your feet up, relax and take your mind off things. The worst part is over, you've made it home. Take off your shoes, pour a cup of tea and forget about your yesterdays. You've got tomorrow to look forward to.

12

The Ten Commandments of Not drinking

1 Never lie about not drinking.

2 Always say straight out: 'I don't drink'.

3 Never be ashamed or embarrassed about not drinking.

4 Always take command of the situation.

5 Time your visits to clubs, pubs, bars and parties.

6 Remember, you don't need to drink to have fun.

7 Tell people only what you want them to know.

8 Never forget why you have given up.

9 If you have to, get help.

10 Say no and keep on saying no.

13

The Test

Are you a sensible social drinker who knows when to stop or do you drink too much? Is your drinking a cause for concern? Should you cut down or even cut it out?

Answer the following questions *honestly* and find out what sort of a drinker you are:

(1) In the past month how many times have you been drunk?
   A 0
   B 1–3
   C More than 3.

(2) In a pub how many drinks in a night do you drink?
   A 1–2
   B 3–4
   C More than 4.

(3) After the pub do you go home and drink more?
   A Never.
   B Sometimes.
   C Often.

(4) Do you have a drink every day?
   A Yes.
   B No.

(5) The morning after the night before do you ever feel:
   A Frightened for no reason?
   B Guilty?
   C Ashamed?
   D Anxious?
   E Embarrassed?

(6) After drinking do you ever suffer from loss of memory?
   A No
   B Yes

(7) Have you ever
    A Tried to give up drinking and failed?
    B Thought about giving up drinking?
    C Neither of these.

(8) Compared to your family and friends, how much do you drink?
    A About the same or less.
    B More.

(9) Have you ever in the last couple of years missed work because of a hangover?
    A Never.
    B Once.
    C More than once.

(10) Has anyone ever commented on how much you drink?
    A Yes.
    B No.

Scores

(1) A1, B3, C5; (2) A1, B3, C5; (3) A1, B3, C5; (4) A5, B1; (5) A5, B3, C5, D5, E3; (6) A1, B5; (7) A5, B3, C1; (8) A1, B5; (9) A1, B3, C5; (10) A5, B1.

If you scored only 1's

Cheers! Your drinking is perfectly harmless and fun. You don't drink too much, don't get drunk and don't have any cause for concern. You know when to stop.

If you scored 1's and some 3's

Your drinking has sometimes let you down and you have been known to push the boat out a bit. Don't let this become a habit. Keep a steady eye on how much you drink and, more important, what effect it has.

If you scored mainly 3's

You are now entering the danger zone. Cut down. You are drinking too much a bit to often and it is beginning to affect your life. Try going without drink. If you can't, seek help.

If you scored 3's and 5's

Like it or not, you have a drink problem. Recognize it or it will only get worse. Drinking is beginning to affect your health and your work. You should seek help straight away.

If you scored mainly 5's

You have a serious problem and deep down you know it. Your health and your work are suffering because of drink. Get some help and stop drinking today. Drink is ripping your apart. Stand up to it and fight back.

PART II

1

Non-alcoholic Drinks

When you give up drinking the big question is what to drink. Here, in this section, are a few ideas, using ingredients available in any High Street supermarket.

One of the most exciting aspects of not drinking is discovering the hundreds of non-alcoholic drinks there are. They can either be drunk on their own or can be mixed together in hundreds of combinations to make long drinks, short drinks, cocktails, summer coolers and winter warmers—the list is endless. Have fun inventing your own.

When looking for new drinks be adventurous and try combinations that might not appear to mix very well, because quite often they do and the result is delicious.

Most soft drinks are best chilled. Use syrups and fruit juices as base drinks and carbonated or fizzy drinks like ginger ale and tonic water as mixers. Soda water and plain and fizzy mineral water make excellent mixers.

Buy small bottles of mixers, ginger, bitter lemon, soda water, ginger beer, etc., because unless you plan to mix up large quantities the bigger bottles will lose their fizz before they are used up.

Remember to use garnishes like cherries, olives, slices of fruit and, when making cocktails, decorate the rim of the glass with coloured sugar or coconut. This is done by adding food colouring to the sugar which is sprinkled on a small plate. The rim of the glass is dipped in water and then into the sugar, coating the rim of the glass. If preferred plain sugar can be used.

If you can afford it, serve the drinks in proper glasses, cocktails in the traditional triangular glasses if they are short drinks, in highball glasses if they are longer drinks. Sparkling drinks can be served in either stemmed goblets or champagne-style long, stemmed glasses. Some drinks which are neither short nor long, tomato juice for example, are best served in medium-sized stemmed glasses or spirit tumblers depending on which feels most comfortable. But if you can't afford them don't worry, you can do without. But don't forget straws: short straws for cocktails, long straws for coolers and highballs.

Besides fruit juices and mixers there are an increasing number of non-alcoholic wines and beers on the shelves. These are good and as long as they are truly non-alcoholic you can drink them without hesitation. But don't use them to disguise your non-drinking. If you do, it's just the same as lying. Don't use these products until you are a confident non-drinker—face up to not drinking first, then go ahead and have fun with them. They have the advantage, especially the beers, of having a more adult taste than fruit drinks.

On the following pages are just a few suggestions for the soft-drink drinker. Try these and invent some for yourself. Above all, have fun.

2

Cocktails

There's no need to feel left out because you don't drink. When you deserve it give yourself a little treat—have a cocktail.

Making cocktails is easy: all you need are a few ingredients you can buy from any corner grocery store. Just a couple of fruit juices and a carbonated mixer like dry ginger is enough to make quite a good selection of different drinks.

With half a dozen fruit juices, a couple of mixers, a cocktail shaker, ice, a few eggs, sugar, and a packet of straws you can hold a fabulous cocktail party and show your friends that drinks don't have to be alcoholic to be delicious.

Here are a few ideas. There are thousands of variations and thousands more new cocktail drinks waiting to be mixed and discovered.

Monkey's Bum

⅓ cherry nectar
⅔ American dry ginger
dash of lime juice cordial

Into a traditional cocktail glass, which has had the rim sugared, pour ⅓ chilled cherry nectar and top up with American, then add just a dash of lime cordial. It is very important not to overdo the lime; there should be just a hint. This is a medium-sweet cocktail.

Passion Wagon

½ passion fruit nectar
soda water
lime juice cordial

This unusual drink really gets the taste buds tingling. Half fill a plain unsugared cocktail glass with chilled passion fruit nectar.

Add a dash of lime juice and fill to the rim with soda water. It can be served with or without an olive. This is a dry, sharp cocktail with a very unusual taste. It feels like the drink is climbing up the back of your teeth and attacking your gums. One of my favourites.

Sweet 'n' Sober

⅓ plum juice
⅓ passion fruit juice
⅓ apricot juice

Mix equal parts of chilled passion fruit, apricot and plum juices in a jug with ice and pour into a cocktail glass decorated with sugar. Serve with a cocktail cherry on a stick. This is one of the simplest of cocktails. A delicious fruity taste, it can be made longer by adding soda water.

Cactus Juice

½ measure cherry nectar
½ measure plum nectar
1 measure American dry ginger
1 egg yolk
ice

For this you need a cocktail shaker, though I do know someone who used an egg cup as a measure and put all the ingredients into a clean milk bottle, which he covered with the palm of his hand to stop it spilling when he shook it.

Put all the ingredients into the shaker and shake until the mixture is cold. Strain into a cocktail glass. This is a delicate cocktail, not too sweet or strong. A family favourite.

Green Apple

½ lime juice cordial
½ apple juice
crushed ice

Into a plain cocktail glass put a couple of crushed ice cubes.

Pour over lime and chilled apple juice. Drink through a straw. This is a strong sharp taste; too sharp for some people.

Pineapple Poll
   2 measures pineapple
   1 egg yolk
   ½ measure single cream
   ice

Put pineapple, egg yolk, cream and ice cubes into a cocktail shaker and give it a good shake. Pour into cocktail glass rimmed with sugar. Decorate with a sprinkling of desiccated coconut. This is a delicious rich, creamy, very sweet, mixture that puts pounds on you by just looking at it. A real favourite, but not for everyday drinking.

Basic Pina Colada
   ⅓ coconut milk
   ⅔ pineapple juice
   ice

Pour ingredients into a cocktail shaker and shake until the mixture is cold and creamy. Strain into a glass. This is one of the most famous of all cocktails. A delicious creamy taste.

Lime Colada
   ⅓ coconut milk
   ⅔ pineapple juice
   fresh lime juice
   ice

Make as for Pina Colada but add a generous dash of freshly squeezed lime juice. The lime gives the drink a sharp after-taste.

Cherry Colada
   ⅓ coconut milk
   ⅔ pineapple juice
   cherry nectar
   ice

Make as for Pina Colada but add a dash of cherry nectar. Serve in a classic-shaped cocktail glass.

Lime Fizz

> ½ measure lime juice cordial
> 1 egg white
> soda water

Put lime juice and egg white into a cocktail shaker and give it a good shake so that the mixture is nice and foamy. Pour the mixture into a cocktail glass and top up with soda. The cocktail should be half soda, half mixture. This cocktail has a real frothy zing and a lovely light texture. A delightful drink. My favourite.

Lemon Fizz

> ½ measure fresh lemon juice
> 1 egg white
> soda water

Make in the same way as Lime Fizz. If the mixture is too sharp, a cube of sugar can be placed in the glass and the mixture poured on top. But it should be pointed out that these are not meant to be sweet cocktails.

3
Coolers and sodas

These are drinks served in highball glasses with plenty of ice. They are especially nice on hot summer days or nights but can be drunk at any time of the year.

Sodas, as their names suggest, are drinks mixed with soda water. They come in a wide range of tastes from very sharp to very sweet. Coolers are long, fruit based drinks often mixed in a jug before serving. Here are a few suggestions.

Basic fruit juice coolers

⅓ orange juice
⅓ pineapple juice
⅓ white grape juice (still)
ice
slices of orange

Mix all three juices and ice in a jug and leave to stand for a couple of minutes. Put slices of orange on top. Pour into individual glasses and garnish each with a slice of fruit. This is a classic fruit drink with a rich fruity taste. Pineapple and orange go well with each other and the grape juice makes the drink that much lighter.

Caribbean Cooler

⅓ orange juice
⅓ mango juice
⅓ guava juice
ice
orange slices

Mix all the ingredients in a jug and leave to stand for two minutes, then pour into individual glasses. Guava juice can be bought tinned or the fruit can be processed in a blender. Mango juice can also be bought in tins and fresh mangos are commonplace.

St Clements

½ orange juice
½ bitter lemon
ice
slices of orange and lemon

This cooler is mixed in the glass. Into a highball glass or lemonade glass put a couple of cubes of ice and add equal measures of fresh orange juice and bottled bitter lemon. Garnish with slices of orange and lemon. Different and delicious.

Passion Cooler

½ passion fruit nectar
½ orange juice
ice
orange slices

Mix ice, fruit juices and orange slices in a jug and leave to stand for two minutes. Pour into individual glasses. Passion fruit has a strong, distinct flavour. You either like it or you don't.

Lemon Lime

4 fresh lemons
4 fresh limes
sugar
ice
Perrier water

Squeeze the juice from the fruit into a jug. Add ice and top up with sparkling Perrier water. Leave for a few minutes and then pour into individual glasses. Add sugar to taste. If there are no fresh fruits available bottled lemon juice can be bought and mixed with a little lime juice cordial. A fresh, sharp taste.

Mint Cooler

⅓ mint tea
⅔ dry ginger
ice

Into a jug pour mint tea mix and top up with dry ginger. Half fill highball glasses with ice cubes and pour the mixture over. Use some mint leaves to decorate.

To make mint tea, brew up some strong tea, pour it into a jug and add a good handful of fresh mint leaves. Leave in the fridge for a couple of hours until the tea has taken a mint flavour.

Toffee Teeth

¼ pineapple juice
¼ apple juice
½ soda water
ice

In a tall glass put a couple of cubes of ice, add equal measures pineapple and apple juice and top up with soda water. Unusual taste.

Orange Soda

½ orange juice
½ soda water

Half fill a tall glass with cold orange juice and top up with soda water. Drink through a straw. One of the most popular pub drinks.

Lemon Press

2 fresh lemons
soda water
sugar
ice

Squeeze the lemons. Put the juice into a tall glass along with a few cubes of ice, add sugar to taste and top up with soda water. This drink should not be over-sugared; keep it sharp.

Lime Press

    2 fresh limes
    soda water
    sugar
    ice

Makes as for lemon Press. Limes are not always in the shops. Keep an eye out for them, and buy whenever possible.

Passion Fruit Soda

    ½ passion fruit nectar
    ½ soda water
    ice

Put ice into a tall glass, add passion fruit nectar and top up with soda water. A strong, dry taste.

Pineapple Soda

    ½ pineapple juice
    ½ soda water
    ice

Make as for Passion Fruit Soda. Fruity and sweet.

Apricot Soda

    ½ apricot nectar
    ½ soda water
    ice

Make as for Passion Fruit Soda. A dry, fruity drink.

Grapefruit Soda

    ½ grapefruit juice
    ½ soda water
    ice

Make as for Passion Fruit Soda. For those who like their drinks bitter, use fresh unsweetened juice.

4

Drinks Containing Grape Juice

Red and white grape juices are delicious drunk on their own. Keep them chilled and drink them just as you would white wine. They can also be mixed with fruit juices, tonic or soda to make before or after dinner drinks.

Here are a few suggestions. Try these and have fun thinking up some fresh ideas for yourself.

Grape 'n' Soda
 ½ red or white grape juice
 ½ soda water

Half fill a wine glass or, if you prefer a longer drink, a tall glass, with grape juice and top up with soda water. This simple drink has the flavour of a light, dry, fruity wine, without a hint of alcohol. Some people prefer a heavier mix of ¾ juice to ¼ soda; it's a matter of taste.

Grape Cassis
 white grape juice
 non-alcoholic cassis or blackcurrant juice

Almost fill a wine glass with chilled white grape juice and top up with cassis or blackcurrant juice. If preferred, sparkling grape juice may be used.

Full Blooded
 ¾ cherry nectar
 ¼ red grape juice

Cherry nectar combines beautifully with both red and white grape juices. This drink, using red juice, has a strong distinct cherry flavour. White grape juice gives the drink a lighter, fruitier texture. This is an excellent after-dinner tipple.

Apricot Aperitif

¼ apricot nectar
¾ white grape juice

Pour the apricot nectar into a wine glass and top up with white grape juice. This is a delicious appetiser, making the taste buds slaver.

Passion Aperitif

¼ passion fruit nectar
¾ white grape juice

Make as for Apricot Aperitif. The distinct flavour of passion fruit gives this drink a real kick.

Tonic and Grape

½ tonic water
½ white grape juice

Into a wine glass pour equal measures of chilled juice and tonic water. This can also be drunk long in a highball glass, in which case add ice. This is a must for lovers of tonic. To be drunk anytime.

Deep Purple

¾ plum nectar
¼ white grape juice

In a wine glass mix together the plum nectar and the grape juice. Serve as an after dinner drink. Tastes a lot lighter than it looks.

Grape Sour

1 large lemon
white grape juice

Squeeze the lemon and pour the juice into a whisky tumbler. Add white grape juice, adjust to taste. The juice should taste sharp with an after-taste of lemon. A good grape sour is a delicate blend, not too grapey, not too lemony.

5

Savoury cocktails

For those people who prefer their drinks savoury here are a few suggestions based on vegetable juices.

Tomato Juice

    1 measure tomato juice
    dash of lemon juice
    Worcester sauce
    Tabasco
    slice of lemon
    ice

The classic drink. Into a medium-sized glass pour a generous measure of tomato juice over a few cubes of ice. Add a squirt of lemon, a drop of Tabasco, a dash of Worcester sauce and a slice of lemon. Stir once and serve.

Snakebite

    ¾ tomato juice
    ¼ orange juice

Mix ingredients in a medium-sized goblet and serve. The orange juice gives the drink a curious sweet and sour taste.

Fool's Gold

    ½ tomato juice
    ½ carrot juice

Make as for Snakebite.

6

Non-alcoholic Beers, Wines, and Spirits

These days it is possible to pour yourself a non-alcoholic pastis or start a meal with a harmless vermouth or campari-type drink. In Australia I even bought a bottle of non-alcoholic whisky.

If you don't fancy a short there is always alcohol-free lager or malt beer or perhaps a little sparkling wine, alcohol-free of course.

Today more and more drinks are being produced with the alcohol taken out. They are so low in alcohol that they are allowed to be declared alcohol-free (there is a little alcohol in them, just as there is alcohol in an apple but it really is negligible). The three terms to look out for on a bottle or can are: alcohol-free, de-alcoholised, or *sans alcool*. Any of these means the drink is safe for consumption. 'Low in alcohol' does not mean the same thing and drinks bearing this legend should be checked out as they will still contain a significant amount of alcohol.

Non-alcoholic tipples should never be used as a substitute for drink but as an alternative. By that I mean you shouldn't hide behind them pretending you're drinking or think of them as substandard alcoholic drinks. They're not. De-alcoholised drinks can never be the same as alcoholic ones and shouldn't be considered in that way; if you do, you haven't really given up drinking. It will only be a matter of time before you are back on the hard stuff. They are an alternative to fruit drinks and have a more sophisticated and adult taste than straight fruit juice or lemonade. Drink them on their own or mix them but always admit they are not alcohol.

Here are just a few alternative beers, wines and spirits and where you can buy them.

Weisslack Extra Dry. A de-alcoholised extra dry white wine produced by taking out the alcohol from a 'real' white wine.

Weisslack. The same as the extra dry but more fruity.

Schloss Boosenburg. A sparkling de-alcoholised white wine excellent on its own or with orange juice in a Bucks Fizz.

Roselack. As its name suggests a de-alcoholised rosé wine. Serve chilled.

Rotlack. De-alcoholised red wine. For those who prefer red to white.

All these are available from Leisure Drinks Ltd, 16 The Green, Aston-upon-Trent, Derby. They can supply a list of stockists in your area or you can order direct.

Americano. A blend of herbs and spices with a curious sweet and sour tang; it is a delightful drink with ice or mixed with ginger or tonic.

Anise. A real French flavour this, the distinctive taste of anise. Drink it with water and imagine you are in Paris.

Bacarat. A big, full flavoured vermouth-type drink without a hint of alcohol. Drink as you would the alcoholic version.

These three drinks are from Katell-Roc of France and are distributed in the UK by Brooke Bond Oxo. Contact Katell-Roc UK at 20 Rock Avenue, Gillingham, Kent.

Kas Bitter. This is a distinctive Campari-coloured bitter alcohol-free aperitif, widely drunk on the continent. It is delicious with ice and lemon or orange slices.

Blancart. This is an alcohol-free pastis produced in France. It has a distinctive yellow-green colour.

Palermo. Available red or white, this is a vermouth-type drink nice on its own or with lemonade.

Panther. This is a non-alcoholic lager beer. It has a nice clean taste, smooth and full-bodied. Panther also make a non-alcoholic malt beer.

All these are available at The Cocktail Shop, 30 Neal Street, Covent Garden, London WC2. The shop boasts one of the most comprehensive stocks of non-alcoholic wines, etc., in the UK.

Barbican. Non-alcoholic lager available in most good off-licences. This is the king of the non-alcoholic drinks. Its clear, dry taste made it an instant hit and its appearance gave rise to the tremendous interest there now is in alcohol-free drinks.